Little Pebble™

Habitats

All About
Deserts

by Christina Mia Gardeski

CAPSTONE PRESS
a capstone imprint

Little Pebble is published by Capstone Press,
1710 Roe Crest Drive, North Mankato, Minnesota 56003
www.mycapstone.com

Library of Congress Cataloging-in-Publication Data
Names: Gardeski, Christina Mia, author.
Title: All about deserts / by Christina Mia Gardeski.
    Description: North Mankato, Minnesota : Capstone Press, [2018] |
    Series: Little pebble. Habitats | Audience: Ages 4–8.
Identifiers: LCCN 2017031565 (print) | LCCN 2017045290 (ebook) |
    ISBN 9781515797692 (eBook PDF) | ISBN 9781515797579 (hardcover) |
    ISBN 9781515797616 (paperback)
Subjects: LCSH: Desert ecology—Juvenile literature. | Deserts—Juvenile literature.
Classification: LCC QH541.5.D4 (ebook) | LCC QH541.5.D4 G368 2018 (print) |
    DDC 577.54—dc23
LC record available at https://lccn.loc.gov/2017031565

Editorial Credits
Marissa Kirkman, editor; Juliette Peters (cover) and Charmaine Whitman (interior), designers;
Eric Gohl, media researcher; Katy LaVigne, production specialist

Photo Credits
Science Source: Tom McHugh, 19; Shutterstock: Anton Foltin, 11, Bildagentur Zoonar GmbH, 12, David Steele,
cover, gkuna, 9, Henderbeth, 1, Lucky-Photographer, 5, Maxim Petrichuk, 7, MicroOne, back cover, interior
(sand dunes illustration), photowind, 15, saiko3p, 17, Stephen Clarke, 21, Zhukov Oleg, 13

Table of Contents

What Is a Desert?

A hot desert is a dry land.

It is made of sand and rocks.

Wind blows the sand.

The sand forms dunes.

dune

Little rain falls here.

It is a dry habitat.

Hot Days

The desert is hot all day.

Cactuses grow in the sun.

Their stems hold water.

Animals adapt.
Camels can go days
without water.
This lizard drinks from
its skin!

thorny devil lizard

Some animals dig down.
A tortoise cools off in
the sand.

Cold Nights

The sun sets.

The desert is cold at night.

Animals come out at night.

Rats run.

Snakes slide.

Owls hunt.

It is time to eat.

Glossary

adapt—to change to fit the land

cactus—a desert plant that stores water in its stems

camel—a desert animal with humps; it can go days without water

dune—a wave of sand blown by the wind

habitat—the home of a plant or animal

lizard—a desert animal with scales, four legs, and a long tail

stem—the part of a cactus that holds water

tortoise—a desert animal with a hard shell and strong legs that digs underground

Read More

Arnold, Caroline. *A Day and Night in the Desert.* Caroline Arnold's Habitats. North Mankato, Minn.: Picture Window Books, 2015.

Riggs, Kate. *Camels.* Seedlings. Mankato, Minn.: Creative Education, 2015.

Ringstad, Arnold. *Desert Habitats.* Habitats. Mankato, Minn.: Child's World, 2014.

Internet Sites

Use FactHound to find Internet sites related to this book.

Visit www.facthound.com

Just type in 9781515797579 and go.

Super-cool stuff!

Check out projects, games and lots more at
www.capstonekids.com

Index